Daydream

Bob J.D. Peters

Illustrated by

Ashley Stanners

Written by Bob J.D. Peters

Illustrated by Ashley Stanners

Edited by Eliza Dee of Clio Editing Services

All rights reserved. No part of this publication may be reproduced, distributed, or transmitted in any form or by any means, including photocopying, recording, or other electronic or mechanical methods, without the prior written permission of the publisher, except in the case of brief quotations embodied in critical reviews and certain other noncommercial uses permitted by copyright law. For permission requests, write to the publisher, addressed "Attention: Permissions Coordinator," at the address below.

permissions@thedaydreambook.com

www.thedaydreambook.com

First Printing, 2016

Copyright © 2016 Bob J.D. Peters

All rights reserved.

ISBN: 9950660-1-4
ISBN-13: 978-0-9950660-1-4

Introduction

We spend half our waking life daydreaming. This book was created to help you get the most out of that time spent. Our minds regularly wander on the trials and tribulations of our daily lives, and you now have the opportunity to change your story, to go beyond everyday daydreams and enter into a new realm of thought and creativity. This book hopes to inspire you through a collection of opportunities and options that will change your status quo.

Thank you for your time and your daydreams.

How to read this book

Setting the right structure for a daydream session will help you get the most out of your time. Ensure you are seated comfortably, minimize distractions and sit back in a comfortable chair. Remember that no one is judging you, no one can see your daydream, and be patient with yourself as you begin this journey. Start by asking yourself the question, what if I relax and enjoy this time daydreaming?

The Scene

The scene is the primary source of information for your daydream. Begin by reading the scene either to yourself or quietly out loud. Close your eyes and begin to envision the scene. Don't be afraid to reread it to view the details on the page. Slowly let yourself sink into the present moment in the scene. Feel the air around you, the sights, the smell, the sounds and the people that you want to take part with you. Like pressing play on a video, the scene will start.

The Options

Not feeling creative? Options are provided to kick-start the beginning of the daydream—use them to ignite your imagination! Each option invites you to daydream in new and creative ways. Combine what you have read in the scene with the options to launch yourself into a scene that could rival a Hollywood blockbuster! What options can you come up with yourself?

The Illustration

After you have spent time daydreaming on the passage, you have the opportunity to view the stylized drawing of each scene that is provided. It will help move you into a whole new way of looking at the scene. Reread the scene again with the illustration in mind. What is different about your daydream this time?

CHAPTER 1
FIREPLACE

The fireplace room is opulent. A number of candelabras help light the warm, shadowy room. A Victorian sofa sits in the middle of the room on top of an ancient hand woven rug edged with yellowing fringe. Heavy oak paneling lines the room, with recessed counters holding crystal decanters and glasses for serving guests. The double entry doors are shut, keeping the warmth of the crackling fire within the room. Crossed swords still in their sheaths sit mounted atop the fireplace. A plush beaver fur blanket sits in a pile on one edge of the sofa.

Options:
1. You help yourself to a drink while waiting for your guest to arrive.
2. You hear a knock at the door and pull one of the swords from its sheath.
3. A crackling spark from the fire sends a hot ember onto the fur blanket.

Daydream

CHAPTER 2

MUSEUM

On top of the central podium stand the fossilized skeletal remains of a dinosaur, its head reaching far up into the ceiling of the building. North, east and west hallways lead into the exhibit areas that promise spectacles and tales of adventures from times past. Next to a row of checkout counters, a velvet rope surrounds a counter for VIP museum members. A large banner hangs down behind the counters, advertising tickets to the Tutankhamen exhibit on display that is combined with a 3-D video of Ancient Egypt. A sign warns against flash photography within the museum.

Options:
1. A person ahead of you in the ticket line offers you a discount coupon to the museum.
2. A tour operator begins to describe the dinosaur fossil in the main hall to a group of tourists.
3. A door is left open to a staff area where you can see a number of precious gems sitting on a table.

Daydream

CHAPTER 3
STREETCAR

The streetcar's antenna reaches up and latches onto a vast network of electrical wires running parallel to metal tracks embedded in the center of the lane. A glowing button sits on the outside of the doors, signaling for a patron to press it to let them in. Inside the streetcar is a ticketing machine with options for cash, tokens and credit. A swipe card system stands at the entryway for regular customers to use. Advertising lines the cabin, with offers of cash for gold and career-programs at local universities. A sectioned off compartment separates riders from the operator.

Options:
1. A local celebrity boards the streetcar and sits down beside you.
2. A rider gets up to exit the streetcar and leaves her purse on the chair.
3. A group of teenagers board the streetcar, singing at the top of their lungs.

Daydream

CHAPTER 4

SHOPPING MALL

Escalators rise up from highly polished floors to a corridor lined with stores. Kiosks fill the middle of the hallway, offering their wares to anyone who may pass by. Light, upbeat music plays over the sound system and fills the background with ambient noise. Rows of revolving doors sit idle at the entranceway to the mall near a large sign advising patrons of where stores are located. An elevator with a large P symbol is open and waiting to descend to the underground parking. A circular fountain shoots water up nearly three stories before it cascades into a pool of shining coins.

Options:
1. You throw a coin into the fountain and make a wish.
2. A newspaper announcing a 90-percent-off sale catches your attention.
3. The lights begin to turn out in each store in a domino sequence.

Daydream

CHAPTER 5

CABANA ON THE BEACH

Salt-, sand- and wind-weathered logs are lashed together with jungle vines that form the frame of the structure. Long, flowing white curtains lift off the ground as the wind from the sea hits them. Thick white pillows fill the inside of the cabana, whose top is completely open to the bright midday sun. The cabana overlooks a beach that stretches as far as the eye can see in each direction. The water changes shades of blue as it extends out into the sea. The smell of coconut suntan lotion still lingers in the air in the cabana, coming from robes hung up to dry at the entrance.

Options:
1. The in-house resort masseuse offers to give you a beach massage.
2. A plastic bucket and shovel left in the sand invite you to build a sandcastle.
3. Off in the distance is a parasail being towed by a speedboat, and it's your turn next.

Daydream

CHAPTER 6
HOTEL ROOM

The hotel room contains pure opulence. There is a hidden flat-screen TV, and an LCD control panel beside the bed controls everything from temperature to the automatic filling of the bathtub. Multiple pillows and a pillow menu rest at the head of the bed, and at the touch of a button, a private butler will be at your beck and call within seconds. A sitting room and dining area separate the bedroom and its en suite bathroom. A tablet computer rather than a binder with brochures lists the hotels many amenities. A fully stocked open bar contains a champagne bucket filled with fresh ice.

Options:
1. You turn on the TV, and a Netflix menu appears allowing you to select your favorite programing.
2. You press the butler button.
3. You press the curtain button on the tablet, and the curtains automatically begin to open, revealing the sun rising over the city of Paris.

Daydream

CHAPTER 7

LAUNDRY ROOM

The apartment building's laundry room is warm and smells sweetly of dryer sheets. Static is in the air from the combination of moisture and warm, dry air. A rumbling sound escapes two of the machines as they whirl through each of their spin cycles. A stack of dryers along the wall with their transparent doors showcase the wardrobe of one of the tenants of the building. Fluorescent lighting panels cast a cool light on leftover boxes of detergent on a folding table that also plays host to a large plastic laundry basket. The floor is a clean, smooth white tile. A single door exits to the basement floor hallway that is lined on each side with bachelor apartments.

Options:
1. A gold diamond ring is inside one of the dryers.
2. The washing machine shuts off prior to the spin cycle, leaving your clothes waterlogged.
3. You open the dryer door and a pair of underwear falls out that are not yours.

Daydream

CHAPTER 8

STADIUM

The dark sky is ringed by bright lights in the open, empty stadium. Everything is perfectly still, including the grass covering much of the ground. White lines stretch across the grass marking each of the yard lines. The seats await the throngs of cheering fans, and the field is ready for the warriors and their cheerleaders in the gladiators' arena. VIP box seats await the rich and famous at midfield. The goalposts rise triumphant, surrounded by a thick cushion. A scoreboard lies dormant, waiting to announce the teams and scores. The doorway to the change rooms stands open, revealing the behind-the-scenes area.

Options:
1. You grab a football and kicking stand and line the ball up for a field goal.
2. A jogger starts running around the track circling the field.
3. The professional football team walks out from the locker.

Daydream

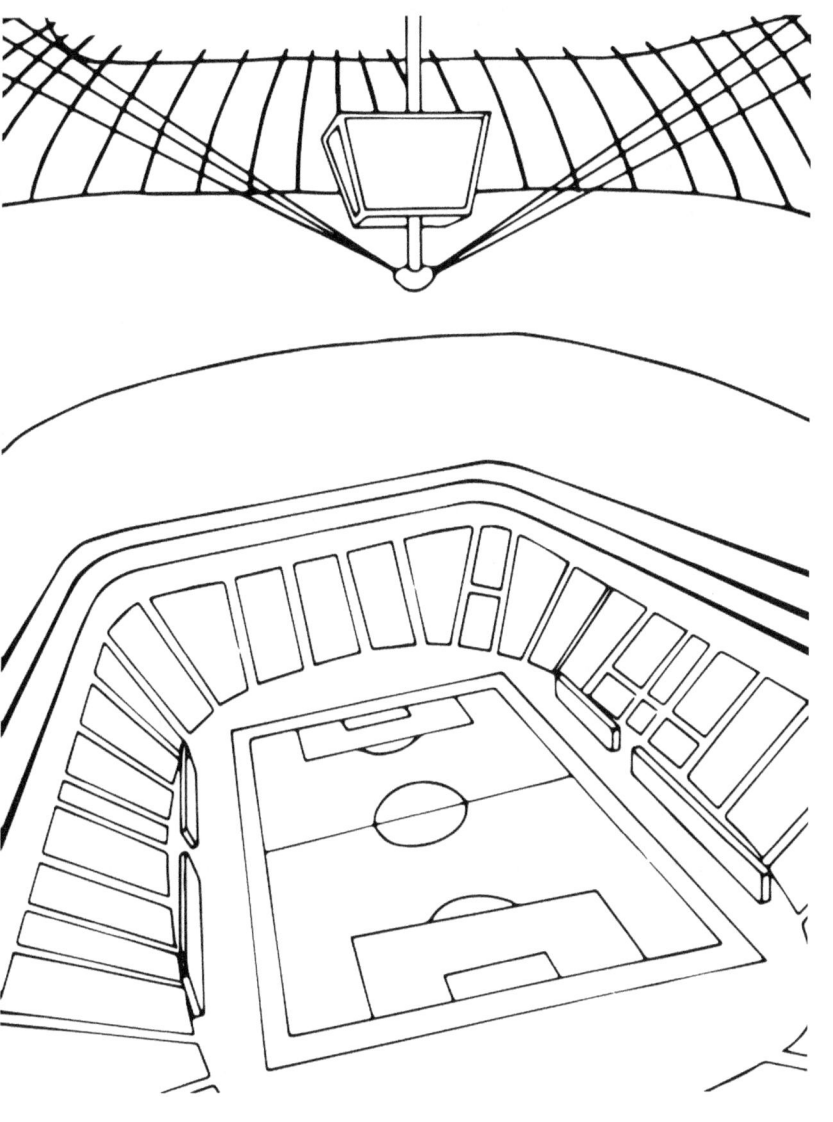

CHAPTER 9
BOOKSTORE

The bookstore's windows are piled with ancient secondhand tomes, many with titles indiscernible from wear or written in a foreign language. A small table piled with books and a handful of chairs sits in the middle of the store for patrons to sit and browse through their finds. Tiny beams of light peer in through the edges of books from the street outside. The smell of leather and well-varnished wood mixes with the scent of old paper and emanates throughout the store. The sound of creaking can be heard as wooden floorboards shift from the cool weather. A sign on the back of the door says "Be back in 15 minutes," ready to be flipped as needed.

Options:

1. A handwritten note sits in between two books of stories from South Africa.
2. What appears to be a first-edition copy of Don Quixote is on sale for one dollar.
3. A teenager opens the antique till and starts filling their pockets with cash.

Daydream

CHAPTER 10

TRAIN

The sleeper cabin is luxurious. One side of the cabin hosts deep bucket chairs with a small table between them. A panoramic window is covered by curtains that close automatically at the press of a button. A sleeper section on the opposite side holds a double bed and an LED television, and there is a bathroom at one end complete with a sink, toilet and shower facility. A minibar offers a selection of wines, glasses, chocolates, peanuts and chips and an ice bucket. The interior is a deep mahogany and smells of old leather. The view out the window is of passing forests and lakes and a mountain range off in the distance.

Options:
1. An invitation to dine with the conductor and enjoy a six-course meal is sitting on the table.
2. The conductor announces that the next stop will be the Banff Springs Hotel.
3. A ticket inspector knocks on the door, but the tickets are no longer in your pocket.

Daydream

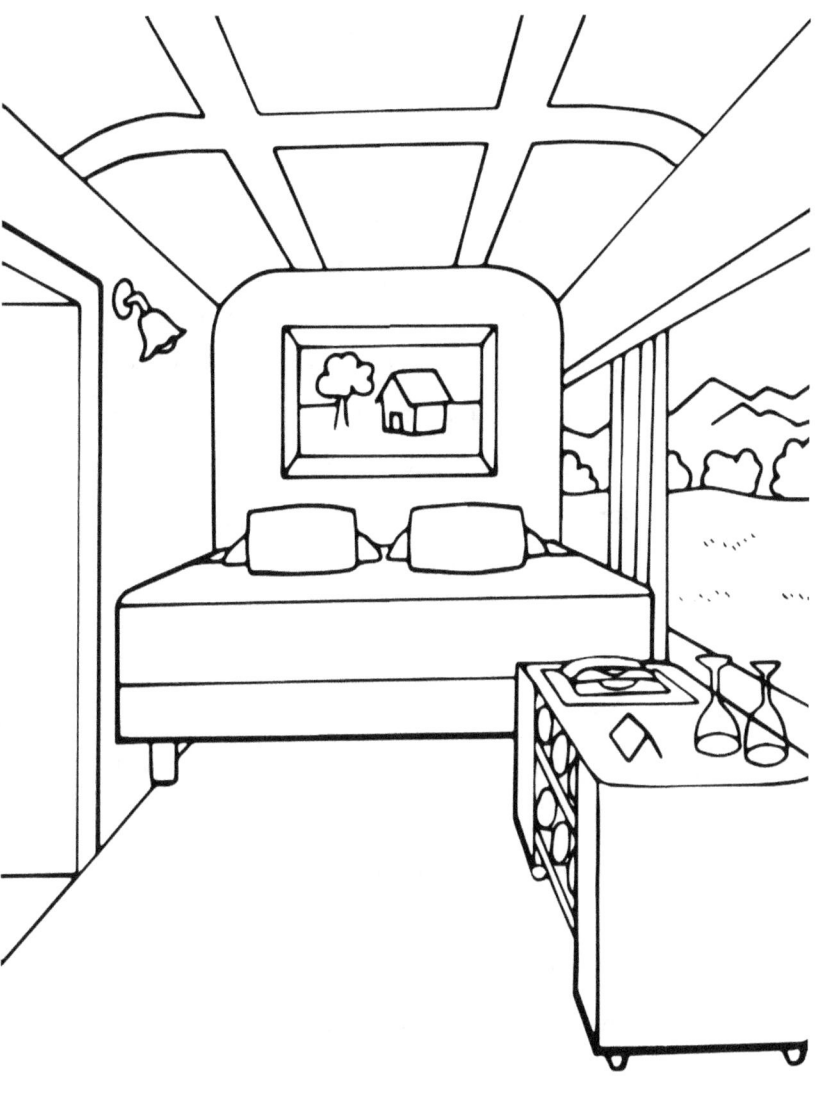

CHAPTER 11

PLANE

Business class in the Boeing 777 is home to lay-flat pods. The left side of the pod contains a package with personal amenities including a toothbrush, socks, bottles of water and noise-canceling headphones. A control panel has buttons to lay the seat perfectly flat like a bed or sit in recliner chair mode or upright for takeoff. In the front of the pod is a large touchscreen LED monitor, and a tray pulls out from the side of the pod when required. A package with a blanket, pillow and pajamas sits on a footrest in the front of the pod.

Options:
1. The flight attendant offers you a glass of French champagne.
2. The "fasten seat belt" sign comes on as the plane encounters severe turbulence.
3. The entertainment system displays an advertisement urging you to connect to Facebook.

Daydream

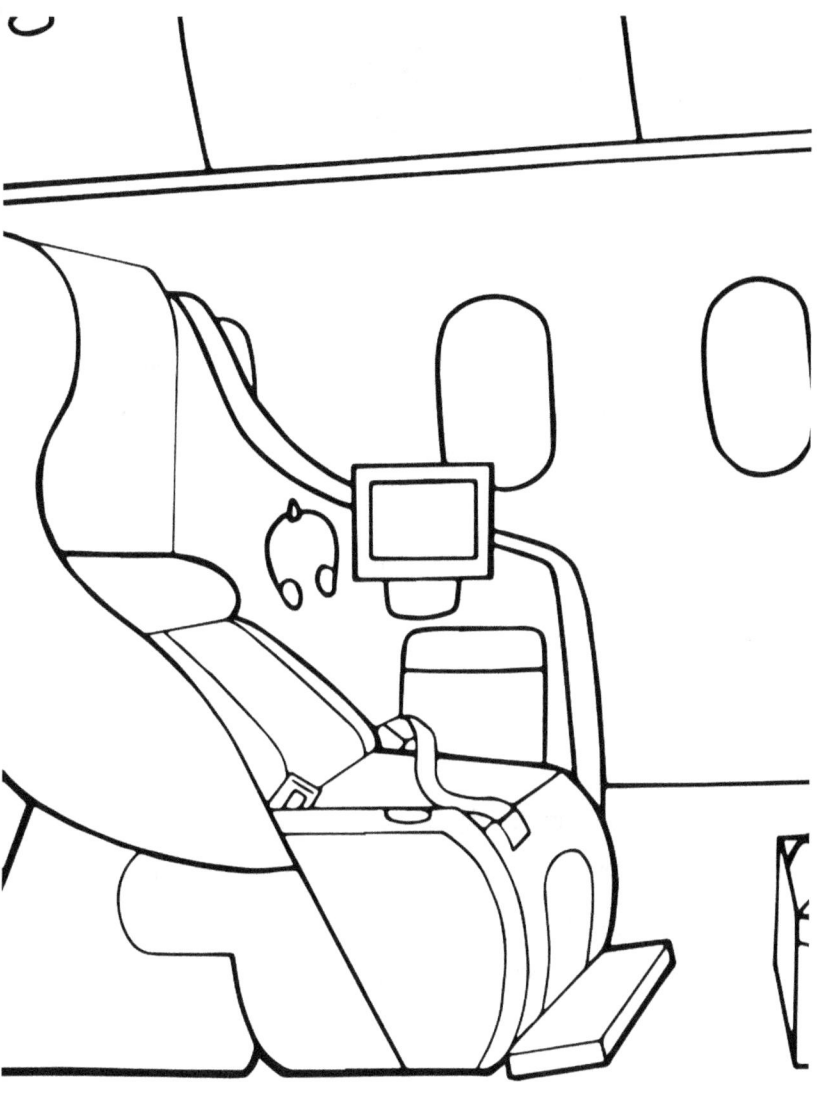

CHAPTER 12

LIMOUSINE

The interior of the limousine is a plush black leather with a large LCD screen underneath the dark glass separator that separates driver and passenger. A minibar along one side of the car houses a selection of bottles and glasses, including wine and harder liquors, as well as an ice bucket. A touchscreen receiver allows control of the devices in the car, including a satellite phone. Nothing can be heard from the outside of the car even though it's parked near a busy intersection. A shaded sunroof is controlled by the touchscreen.

Options:
1. A bicyclist clips the driver's-side mirror.
2. The driver informs you that you are one block away from the concert.
3. A video conference call alert pops up on the screen.

Daydream

CHAPTER 13

ARCADE

The arcade is filled with overwhelming sounds coming from dozens of machines lined up like soldiers along the arcade walls. The dimly lit room plays host to claw-type games with stacks of stuffed animals. A retro corner houses pinball machines from decades past. A bill converter station stands at the entrance to the arcade, ready to convert cash into tokens. A bar runs the length of one of the walls, ready to serve finger food and adult beverages. Diner-style booths contain retro games in place of what would have been a mini jukebox. In the back of the room is a row of racing car pod games, ready to challenge any competitors.

Options:
1. A DJ announces that every night is 80s night and begins to play music.
2. A teddy bear is sitting half on the edge of the prize chute in the claw game.
3. A classic arcade game competition offers the arcade cabinet of the winner's choice as the first-place prize.

Daydream

CHAPTER 14

AMUSEMENT PARK RIDE

The roller coaster has twists and turns and double loops. The cars seat four people each, with a harness that pulls down over the top of the riders' shoulders to secure them in place. Long aisles are sectioned off by metal gates, and there is a compartment to put your belongings in so that they don't fly off on the ride. The first hill rises higher than is visible within the loading area, and the smell of freshly popped popcorn fills the air. A pathway on the other side of the track leads the people who have finished the ride back into the main park area.

Options:

1. The small passenger next to you asks to hold your hand.
2. A grinding sound can be heard as the cars stall at the apex of the tallest hill.
3. Your cell phone falls out of your pocket and onto the floor of the roller-coaster car.

Daydream

CHAPTER 15

PUBLIC POOL

A twenty-foot-high wired fence lines the outskirts of the public swimming pool. Life preservers and flutterboards hanging on each side of three shaded lifeguard stands. The deep end features a high diving board with a ladder climbing up to the diving platform and a lower ground-level springboard. The shallow end is marked with signs that say "No Diving" and "No Running." A nearby entranceway marks the men's and ladies shower and change rooms. A floating rope barrier separates the shallow end from the deep end of the pool. The water temperature is very cold compared to the warm air and beaming sunshine, and there is a strong odor of chlorine.

Options:
1. You stand at the edge of the high diving platform looking down into the clear, cold water.
2. An aqua exercise class is about to begin in the shallow end of the pool.
3. A whistle is blown, alerting everyone to leave the pool immediately.

Daydream

CHAPTER 16
OCEANSIDE

A white concrete pathway weaves its way through the sand alongside the beach. The sound of waves can be heard washing up on the shore close by. Colorful umbrellas dot the edge of the pathway, offering shade from the overpowering sunshine. Small shops offering tourist memorabilia are open to the street. A restaurant patio sits closed, waiting for the lunch crowd. A red flag cautions swimmers of the rough seas and strong undertow. A dark patch of clouds off in the distance is heading towards the shore. The smell of rain is in the air.

Options:
1. You wade into the water up to your knees as the sand pulls at your feet.
2. A Segway tour starts at 2 p.m.
3. Store owners shutter their windows and pull in umbrellas and goods from outside.

Daydream

CHAPTER 17
COTTAGE

Bright red "No Trespassing" signs line the edge of the dense forest surrounding the enclosed cottage beach. A long wooden dock extends out into the shallow, murky waters. The dock creaks as the waves tap at its timbers. Ropes hang from the slips used for mooring a boat. A single chair sits at the end of the dock with a fishing pole leaned up against it and a tackle box at its feet. The smell from an extinguished campfire is present in the air. An overturned canoe sits near the top of the beach underneath a group of trees where it is tethered to a tree by a metal chain.

Options:
1. A loon dives into the water for a fish.
2. An open bag of marshmallows and roasting sticks sit near the campfire.
3. A boat is floating empty in the lake.

Daydream

CHAPTER 18

MANSION

A high black iron-barred gate surrounds the sweeping home. A fountain stands in the middle of the property, shooting jets of water into the air, creating its own rainbow effect across the front of the property. The grass is well manicured around the front of the home, with pathways weaving into gardens and a hedge maze. Songbirds can be heard as they nest in the large oak trees in front of the home, and the sounds of horses come from the attached stables. A black paved driveway leads up to a massive entranceway framed in ornately carved columns. A side entrance leads down to an underground parking area. On the other side of the driveway rests a grass tennis court surrounded by a high fence and a cabana.

Options:
1. You sit in the swing hanging from the oak tree.
2. You pick up a bucket of feed and a horse comb and head towards the stables.
3. Keys to an Italian-made super car are in the ignition.

Daydream

CHAPTER 19
HOT TUB

A sheen of steam floats up into the cold air from the surface of the bubbling water. Mounds of snow are gathered around the wooden encasement, hiding all but a slim shoveled pathway leading to the hot tub. A barbecue covered with snow sits on a long stone table connected to the hot tub. Snow-covered evergreens create a privacy screen around the edge of the property. The sounds of birds chirping float softly into the environment, blending in with the hum of the hot tub jets firing streams of water that breach the surface.

Options:
1. You climb into the hot tub and press the "play music" button on its control panel.
2. You lift the hood to the barbecue and start it up.
3. The hot tub jets begin shooting out cold water.

Daydream

CHAPTER 20
CANDY STORE

Candy-dispensing tubes line a wall filled with brightly colored candy-coated peanuts. Rows of shelves are stocked with candy-filled baubles and trinkets. A candy machine sits in the middle of the room, waiting for its gumdrop handle to be pulled and candy to be dispensed for a nominal fee. The walls are yellow and the floor a pristine white. The cool air keeps everything at an appropriate temperature. A candy taste-testing area is situated in the back of the store with inlaid candy-serving dishes along a long wooden communal table.

Options:
1. You put a quarter into the candy machine and pull the handle.
2. A tray is sitting on the counter offering free samples.
3. You walk up the stairs leading to the second floor milkshake and ice cream soda bar.

Daydream

CHAPTER 21

UNDERGROUND PARKING

Cool blue fluorescent lights in the ceiling of the parking garage illuminate rows of numbered parking spaces. Cement columns are dispersed around the floor with location colors and numbers. Signs point towards a steel exit door and a stairwell leading out of the underground parking. A ramp continues down deeper underground. The sound of water dripping comes from pipes in the ceiling which drip water onto the ground from the humidity. One of the cars still has its lights on, illuminating one of the walls in a white light. The entrance to the elevator is blocked by an "out of service" sign.

Options:
1. A chirping sound comes from a car whose alarm is enabled.
2. You reach into your pocket to open your car door, but you are missing your keys.
3. Two people are talking in hushed tones near a black SUV.

Daydream

CHAPTER 22

OFFICE BUILDING

Rows of cubicles with computer monitors face high-backed office chairs. An industrial-sized printer with multiple paper tray shelves separates the floor into two halves. A digital dashboard streams information, showing the current date. Exposed brick walls lead up to hanging pot lights, only half of which are on. The kitchen is dark at this time of night, save for the flashing lights on the microwave ovens. Meeting rooms with large screens and long tables and walls lined with whiteboards sit empty. Executive offices with their window views have their doors closed and locked.

Options:
1. A computer is on and logged in to one of the staff members' Facebook account.
2. A file sitting in the locked executive office is marked strictly confidential.
3. A security guard asks how your day is going.

Daydream

CHAPTER 23

CONSTRUCTION SITE

The perimeter of the site is enclosed by twelve-foot-high fences covered in plywood. A portal cut in one of the plywood fences provides a view of the construction area. The first two floors are illuminated by large spotlights casting dark shadows into the inner workings of the building. The cold climate has icicles hanging off the sides of the portable office, and whiffs of steam can be seen coming out of the portable's rooftop vent. Piles of steel bars, cement-mixing machines and wheelbarrows are strewn about the caged-in grounds, being carefully watched over by a security guard in a booth.

Options:
1. You enter the temporary elevator and press the up button.
2. The security guard asks to see your identification.
3. The guard dog walks in front of you.

Daydream

CHAPTER 24
SCIENCE CENTER

The main hall in the science center opens up into three branching archways, labeled Past, Present and Future. Monuments of Thomas Edison, Albert Einstein and Neil Armstrong each sit guarding the center of each exhibit entranceway. The ceiling is illuminated by lights symbolizing constellations. Velvet ropes corral ticket purchasers in front of booths. A sign for a 3-D Mars flight simulator lists today's schedule. The floor is a gleaming white marble that reflects the lighting from the ceiling, creating a spotlight effect on the ground. Rows of headsets sit behind the check-in desk, offering audio tours to guests. Signs point towards the men's and women's bathrooms.

Options:
1. You walk towards the indoor tornado exhibit.
2. An unfinished equation fills a chalkboard.
3. You receive the last two tickets for the day to the Mars 3-D exhibit.

Daydream

CHAPTER 25
ZOO

High glass walls line the edge of the polar bear cage, which features an entranceway into the swimming area and a slide into a pool filled with ice-cold water. The pool continues deep underground to a viewing area for visitors to view the bears diving underwater. A snow-covered motif adorns the back wall. Signs are posted around the pool warning visitors not to tap on the glass, feed the animals or use flash photography. Visitors are directed to venture down below and visit the gift shop for official polar bear souvenirs.

Options:
1. A child asks how the polar bears are able to breathe underwater.
2. The zookeeper walks out from the polar bears' cave.
3. You tap on the glass.

Daydream

CHAPTER 26
RESTAURANT

Silverware sparkles underneath the central chandelier suspended overhead. Pristine white plates are stacked on top of white tablecloths, with artfully folded napkins in their center. Sliding doors at one end separate off the private dining suite. A central glass-enclosed wine cellar is lined with bottles from floor to ceiling. The smell of chargrilled steaks is wafting through the room. The salad bar contains an assortment of toppings, dressings and freshly made croutons together with large pots containing the soup of the day. White dishes line each end of the salad bar, which is covered by a long pane of glass.

Options:
1. The menu items are all written in Japanese.
2. Your reservation is delayed by 20 minutes.
3. The sounds of an argument are coming from the kitchen.

Daydream

CHAPTER 27

WEDDING RECEPTION

The entrance to the reception hall is adorned with white balloons arranged in the shape of a heart for guests to pass through. A table for guests to leave presents and gift cards sits just inside the hall entranceway. Before the entranceway, there sits a coat check area with the lights turned off. A staircase leads to the lower level, where the washrooms are located. Swinging doors with circular windows lead off to the stainless steel kitchen. A table covered with miniature white roses sits waiting for the ceremonial cake to arrive. Tables with numbered stands on them are bare, with no tablecloths or place settings. A DJ table is surrounded by crates of records.

Options:
1. One of the balloons pops behind you.
2. Streaming water is coming from under the kitchen door.
3. The bride asks you where the tablecloths and place settings are.

Daydream

4.

CHAPTER 28

RESORT

Warm, humid air blows through the lobby of the resort. At the entranceway, a statuesque fountain sends multiple streams of water up into the air, delivering a cool mist to the surrounding manicured garden. Multiple clocks reside on the wall, showing an array of international time zones. An automatic sliding door opens into the lobby's twenty-four-hour bar, complete with large-screen TVs playing today's sporting events. Palm tree leaves swaying in the breeze can be viewed from the deep-cushioned lounges in the panoramic open lobby. A store selling small goods invites guests in with the promise of half-off sales.

Options:
1. A server offers you a welcome beverage.
2. You walk into the store and look for new sunglasses.
3. The football world cup is on in the sports bar.

Daydream

CHAPTER 29
PARK

A flower bed surrounds the smooth wooden park bench with curved black metal arms extending from each of its sides. A garbage bin sits on one side, offering sections for garbage and recycling. A duck pond with lily pads and a fountain is in close view from the park bench. Luminous white clouds dot the sky, creating shadows over sections of the park grounds. Tulip bulbs are starting to sprout from the earth in the flower beds. The muted city hum from the urban center creeps into all areas of the park. Beyond the pond sits an empty baseball diamond waiting for spring season to finally arrive.

Options:
1. Your team sets up in the baseball diamond for practice.
2. You bring a half loaf of bread to feed the ducks.
3. A horse-drawn carriage offers 50 percent off morning rides through the park.

Daydream

CHAPTER 30

PLAYGROUND

Smooth white pebbles provide a soft bedding for the playground area. A maze of tubes runs through the center of the playground with chain ladders leading up to the top of a tube slide that twists in a spiral down to the ground. Separate swings grind against their hanging supports in the gentle summer breeze. Wooden park benches surround the playground while a single bench sits underneath the canopy of a large maple tree. A drinking fountain dribbles out water along a pathway which leads to a small railed-in parking lot. An overfull garbage can sits at the end of the pathway at the edge of the parking lot.

Options:
1. You sit down on the swing.
2. A Frisbee lands at your feet.
3. A car playing deep bass music pulls into the playground parking lot.

Daydream

CHAPTER 31
COFFEE SHOP

Two long wooden communal tables sit in front of the floor-to-ceiling windows in the coffee shop. Wide-open doors welcome visitors to smell the brewing lattes and espresso shots coming from within. An eclectic mix of chairs and benches sit around the tables, while a variety of kinds and colors of mugs sit on wooden shelves. A selection of pastries are displayed on an old-fashioned cake tray with a tall glass lid. Exposed brick walls and ductwork show signs of the original industrial use of the building. A stack of daily newspapers from around the world sits at the end of the counter available for patrons to read.

Options:
1. Kopi Luwak coffee is the day's current feature.
2. The barista hands you your coffee in a mug shaped like the Eiffel Tower.
3. You talk with the shop owner about selling your homemade butter tarts in the store.

Daydream

CHAPTER 32

HOUSE FOR SALE

An open house sign sits at the front of a long, wide concrete driveway, which is devoid of any vehicles. There are two large planters sitting at each side of the entranceway. A large maple tree is in the front yard, its leaves beginning to turn into fall colors. The garage door is open, revealing a space lit only by a single light on the automatic garage door opener, empty save for a door leading into the home and a central vacuum system. A round second-story window is open and dance music can be heard from within the room.

Options:

1. The real estate agent knocks on the door.
2. You walk into the garage and open the house door and ask if anyone is home.
3. The garage door closes and the front door opens.

Daydream

CHAPTER 33
TREE ON A HILL

A lone tree sits on top of a hill. Thick, strong branches extend out from its wide base, creating a natural ladder to climb up into its far reaches. The ground below the tree has thick green grass nestled right up to the base of the trunk. The view of small farmers' fields growing flowers can be seen for miles. The sweet smell of pollen is in the air, mixed with the rich, earthy tones from the tree branches. The leaves are full and cover the ends of each branch, creating a natural umbrella. Sweet, sticky sap is running down from one of the knots on the tree.

Options:
1. A child pulling a wagon is selling fresh flowers.
2. A branch snaps and comes falling down from above.
3. You look down at your wedding ring and remember that this is where the proposal occurred.

Daydream

CHAPTER 34
DOG PARK

Wood chips and gravel coat the floor of the enclosed area. A multilevel water fountain with a ground level spout sits in the middle of the grounds. Spring-loaded entryways have garbage and recycling containers within a close distance. Signs remind pet owners to pick up after their pets while in the area. A section of car tires buried vertically in the ground at different levels give the opportunity for perches and obstacles. The shoulder-high fence surrounding the area provides no chance for all but the smallest animals to escape. A slightly mangled tennis ball sits beside a bench seat.

Options:
1. A small dog prances in front of a ball at your feet.
2. One of the dog owners neglects to pick up after their pet.
3. A high-pitched yelp comes from the obstacle course.

Daydream

CHAPTER 35

SUBWAY PLATFORM

Fluorescent lights hum above the tracks, casting a hard blue light over the platform. Posters on the walls detail specials at nearby restaurants and feature glossy photos of featured dishes. An emergency crisis phone attached to a box on a column offers help to those in need. Yellow markings along the walkway warn travelers to stand back from the edge. The sports section from a daily newspaper sits at the end of a courtesy bench. An escalator with an out-of-service barrier in front of it leaves patrons no other choice than to walk up a long flight of stairs.

Options:
1. A street musician begins playing Beethoven.
2. You realize that the train you just boarded is heading in the wrong direction.
3. The emergency phone receiver is off the hook, and a voice repeating the word hello can be heard coming from it.

Daydream

CHAPTER 36
TAXI

The taxi is parked alongside an old brick building with inches between the passenger door and the wall. The driver's door was left wide open, the headlights turned on, highlighting droplets of rain tapping on a puddle. A fire escape ladder is pulled down to the ground behind the taxi, leading up to a series of zigzagging platforms that scale the brick wall up ten stories. The empty taxi still has the radio playing and the keys left in the ignition. A closed black briefcase sits on the backseat of the taxi. The meter is still running in the cab.

Options:
1. The taxi cab driver asks you for a light.
2. Someone from behind you tells you to get in and drive.
3. You grab the briefcase and run.

Daydream

CHAPTER 37

MOVIE THEATER

The smell of popcorn extends well into the street amid bright lights surrounding the title of the films playing in the theater. Open doors on both sides of the ticketing booth show a warm, inviting interior and concession stand. The sound of popcorn popping inside enclosed glass cases competes with the room-shaking bass from the movie playing in the auditorium. Closed doors block the way into the two rooms playing feature movies. Stairways with "Do Not Enter" signs draped across them lead to an upper balcony area in the theater that remains from its earlier days as an opera house. A scattering of popcorn kernels sits on the floor in front of the concession stand, partly ground into the carpet.

Options:
1. The manager hands you the broom and tells you to do your job and clean up the mess.
2. You walk into the Do Not Enter area.
3. The "Sold Out" sign is turned on for the feature movie.

Daydream

CHAPTER 38

DUNGEON

Narrow stone steps lead down into the depths of the dungeon. The smell of damp moss emanates from rocks. In the center of the room, suspended from the ceiling, is an oversized birdcage large enough for a person to fit in. The walls have chains and shackles hanging from them. Wind enters through the cracks in a large wooden door at the entrance, whistling and blowing fine sand. A chair with shackles and a vise at the arms and legs is made out of a smooth wood. The room is illuminated by buzzing lights. A velvet rope keeps tourists from entering any further into the room. The sound of water dripping can be heard from the back of the dungeon.

Options:
1. Your guide cautions you to watch your step on the slippery floor.
2. The birdcage falls to the ground and shatters.
3. You feel a hand on your back and turn around to see that no one is there.

Daydream

CHAPTER 39
KITCHEN

Gleaming white floors reflect an array of pot lights that shine down from the ceiling and surround an open window skylight. An L-shaped central island hosts a dual sink next to gas burners and a griddle. The fridge is recessed into the wall with a collection of magnets and notes on its front. Open cupboards showcase a selection of bone-white china, suitable for a dozen guests. Wineglasses hang upside down from the bottom of the cupboards in mounting brackets. A wooden cutting board sits on the kitchen counter next to a knife block with a collection of razor sharp knives.

Options:
1. Your friendly neighbor brings over a bottle of wine and a movie.
2. Guests are waiting for you to begin serving dinner.
3. Rainwater begins to seep in through the open skylight.

Daydream

CHAPTER 40
CAR GARAGE

The doors to the double-wide garage are open, raised up on motorized tracks under the ceiling. Metal lockers filled with gardening implements are propped open by partially filled red gas cans. A wheelbarrow filled with chopped wood sits near the side exit door. Black stains on the cement floor showcase where time has been spent repairing vehicles. The smell of oil comes from a pair of coveralls hanging from a hook on the wall. Tools are neatly placed along the top of a workbench, each with its own specific place. Tin cans on a metal shelf are filled with various screws, nails and widgets.

Options:
1. A small child asks you to fix their bicycle.
2. You put on the coveralls and drive your car into the garage.
3. The button that closes the garage door stops working.

Daydream

CHAPTER 41

BROADWAY PLAY

The rafters are lined with scaffolding that crisscrosses the stage, with elements ready to be dropped into the scenes of the show. Lighting elements attached to remote-controlled motorized boxes allow any spot on the stage to be pinpointed and bathed in color. Exits on the sides of the stage lead to multiple hallways that contain dressing rooms and alcoves filled with the show's costumes. Monitors display the show to the crew and give them instant visual access to the stages of the play. Tunnels underneath the stage end in trapdoors for visual spectacles and on-stage surprises. A sign sits above the stage door exit, displaying the message, "You either have it, or you've had it."

Options:
1. The lead actress refuses to go on stage.
2. People are sitting in your reserved seats.
3. The trapdoor opens above you, and you are lifted up through the stage floor and in front of the audience.

Daydream

CHAPTER 42

WATER PARK

In the splash pad, fountains of water shoot up from the ground in a turbulent spout more than ten feet in the air. Soft ribbed material lines the area, sparing individuals from slipping on the watery surface. Small holes in the material drain the water into the pumping stations below the surface. A collection of colorful air mattresses at a convenience stand sit idle, waiting for their next dip in the nearby heated pool. A wall of water cascades from an outpouring in an artificial waterfall, its architecture mirroring a rocky outcropping. Multiple waterslides intertwine and exit into a small pool monitored on each side by lifeguard stations.

Options:

1. A jet of water from the splash pad knocks your glasses off and up into the air.
2. You paddle on the air mattress towards the waterfall.
3. You walk up to the top of the world's fastest waterslide.

Daydream

CHAPTER 43
TREE HOUSE

The ladder leading up to the tree house advises guests that there are "no adults allowed" on the premises. A hatch at the top of the ladder is open into the main level, which sports an intercom system between it and the main home. A cardboard box of toys sits beside a small table with stools. A butterfly net is next to a group of mason jars with holes poked in the lids and the remnants of various insects inside. A second ladder leads up to the roof of the tree house, where a telescope lets guests look at the stars and match them up to a star map posted on the tree.

Options:
1. Tonight, Mars and Venus are viewable in the night sky.
2. A voice over the intercom asks what's for dinner.
3. There is an animal in the tree house chirping at you.

Daydream

CHAPTER 44
CLOTHING STORE

A photograph on the wall depicts a woman without expression looking into the distance behind sunglasses. Below her stands a mannequin wearing a similar jacket to that worn by the one in the photograph. Carousels of clothing are arranged without any seeming pattern. Signs lead towards the checkout counter and numbered change rooms. An escalator leads down to the ground floor, where ladies' perfumes and jewelry are located. All clothing pieces have attached security monitoring devices that beep when customers attempt to leave the store with them still attached. Upbeat music is playing on the store speaker system to help lift customers' spirits.

Options:
1. A sign lists all fall fashion items as 80 percent off.
2. The lock on the change room door is broken.
3. A security monitoring device sets off the store alarm as you walk through the exit door.

Daydream

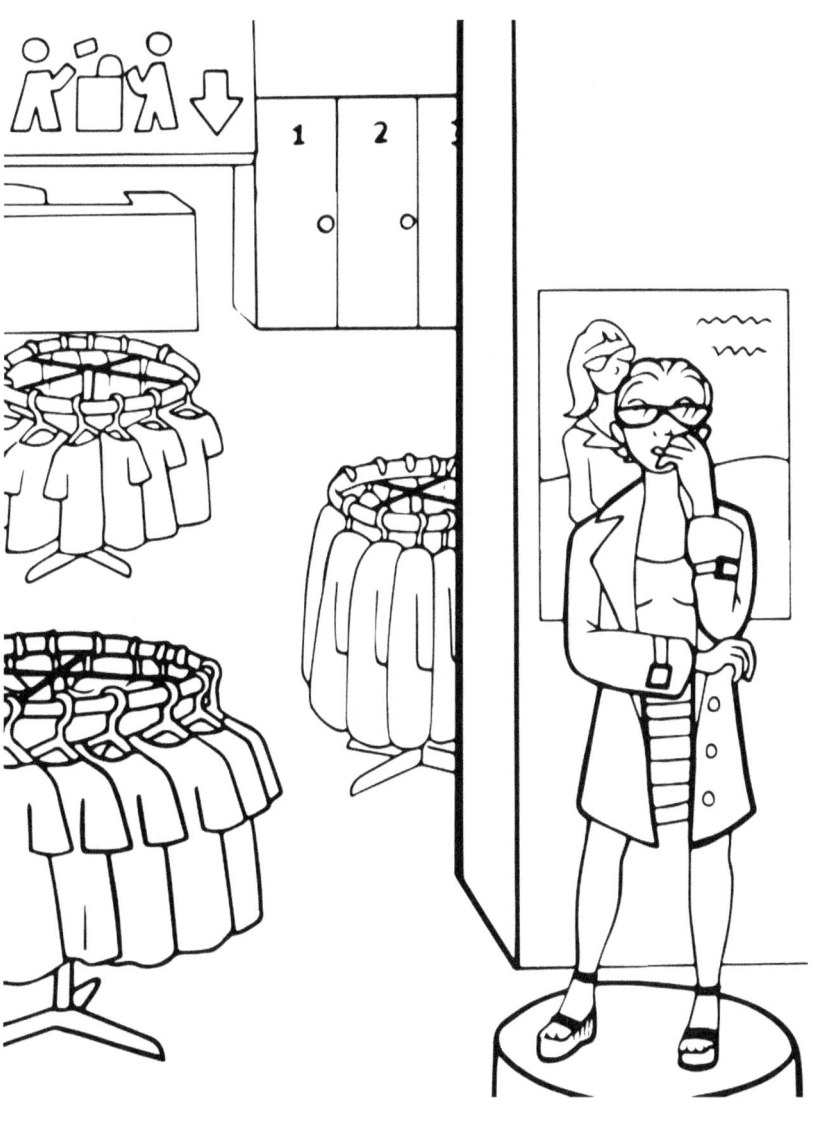

CHAPTER 45
LIGHTHOUSE

Waves crash against an outcropping of gray rocks leading into the tumultuous sea. A seventy-foot drop extends from the edge of the rock ledge to the rolling waves below. The lighthouse lights are on, excluding the flood light sitting at the top observation deck. An iron railing surrounds the top deck, while the wooden platform shows wear and tear from the elements. A single bench beside the lighthouse is covered in graffiti and hand-carved initials. A single-lane driveway leads away from the lighthouse into the surrounding forested area. A "Do Not Enter" sign posted on the door to the lighthouse is lightly knocking against the door from the ocean breeze.

Options:
1. The lighthouse door is unlocked.
2. A car pulls up directly behind yours in the driveway.
3. As you step on the wooden platform, a board cracks and splinters under your foot.

Daydream

CHAPTER 46
ART GALLERY

The unconventional art wing of the gallery features the transformation of everyday items into artistic sculptures. Up on the second floor of the art gallery is an intact upside-down World War II helicopter resting on rotary blades in the shape of a peace sign. At the top of the stairs is a collection of galloping horses crafted from glue bottles, complete with red plastic horseshoes. A collection of lights shines against a two-story house made out of playing cards, complete with a living room, dining room and upper-floor bedroom. Numbers assigned to each exhibit correspond to codes for a self-guided audio tour of the exhibits.

Options:
1. A student is sitting on a bench sketching.
2. You press the corresponding audio code beside the playing cards exhibit.
3. A security guard stands beside the house of cards, watching passersby.

Daydream

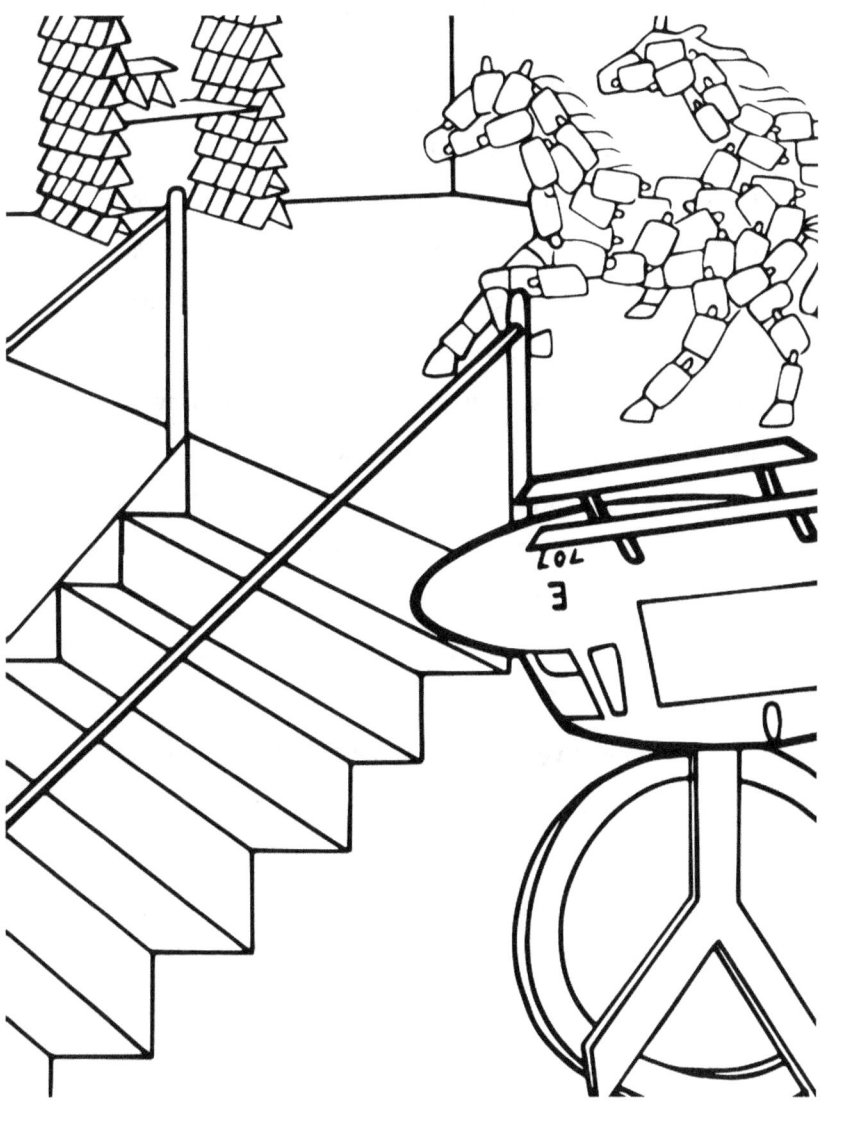

CHAPTER 47

GYMNASIUM

The sound of humming coming from the lights is present in the room. Regulation-height basketball hoops sit at either end of the room, their mesh nets hanging down from orange rims attached to Plexiglas backboards. An elevated stage sits behind the basketball hoop at one end of the room. The backboard can be raised or lowered on a pulley system for a clear view of the stage. A storage room beside the stage is open, and inside are three large foam crash mats, volleyball poles and a storage shelf with a collection of volleyballs, basketballs and dodgeballs.

Options:
1. You grab five balls and set up the room for dodgeball.
2. You set up the crash mat near the front of the stage.
3. Coach wants you in the starting lineup for tonight's volleyball championship.

Daydream

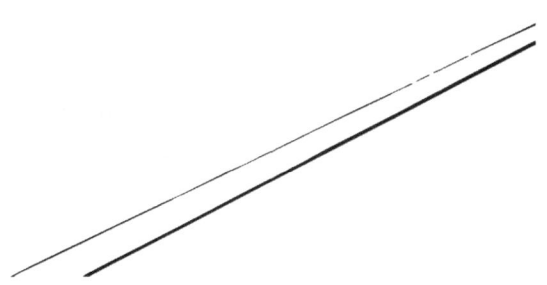

CHAPTER 48

POLICE STATION

A cold, hard metal tab is bolted to the floor in the middle of the room. Scratch marks are etched on the surface of the table and table legs where individuals have been handcuffed before. A small four-by-four-inch window of shatterproof glass is set in the heavy door. A video camera is connected above the door, its light flashing red. A two-way mirror that spans the length of the room allows for discussions to be monitored and viewed privately. A steaming cup of hot coffee in a plain paper cup sits on the table.

Options:

1. You enter the room, and a person sitting at the table asks if you are their lawyer.
2. On the other side of the two-way mirror, an officer asks you to identify the perpetrator.
3. The red light on the camera goes out as the door opens.

Daydream

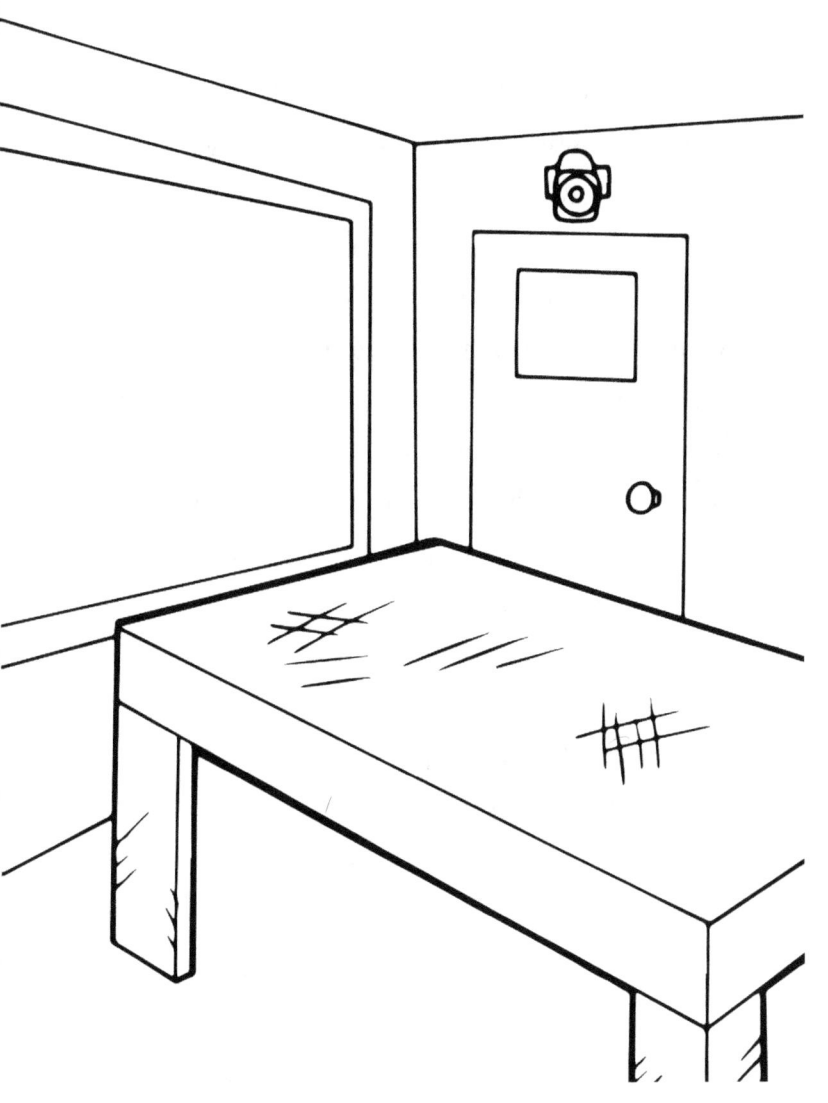

CHAPTER 49
BOARDROOM

Large high-backed leather chairs with leather arms surround the oval table. Smaller chairs sit against the walls of the room for those playing supportive roles in meetings. A large television sits at one end of the room with a video camera sitting on top of it that points down towards the table. A whiteboard covers the length of one wall, and a collection of markers sits on a shelf at its bottom. An audio-video telephone system LCD panel sits at one end of the table with controls for all of the room's systems. Artistic paintings provide the only glimpse of the outside world in the room.

Options:
1. You press the button to open the curtain.
2. The conference phone rings.
3. Members of the board take their respective seats around you.

Daydream

CHAPTER 50
ELEVATOR

Inside the elevator are buttons labeled from 35 to 55, along with emergency, call and stop buttons. Two digital screens highlight the weather and current news stories, with stock exchange information scrolling across the bottom. The mirrored walls of the elevator give the small compartment a larger feel. Warm lighting emanates from multiple pot lights shining on the waist-high polished wooden handrail. A service mode keyhole sits underneath the grating for the elevator speaker. Soft music plays within the elevator, interrupted only by the robotic voice announcing arrival at the ground floor.

Options:
1. A small child asks to press the floor buttons.
2. A delivery person walks in holding a bouquet of flowers.
3. The elevator stops before reaching the ground floor.

Daydream

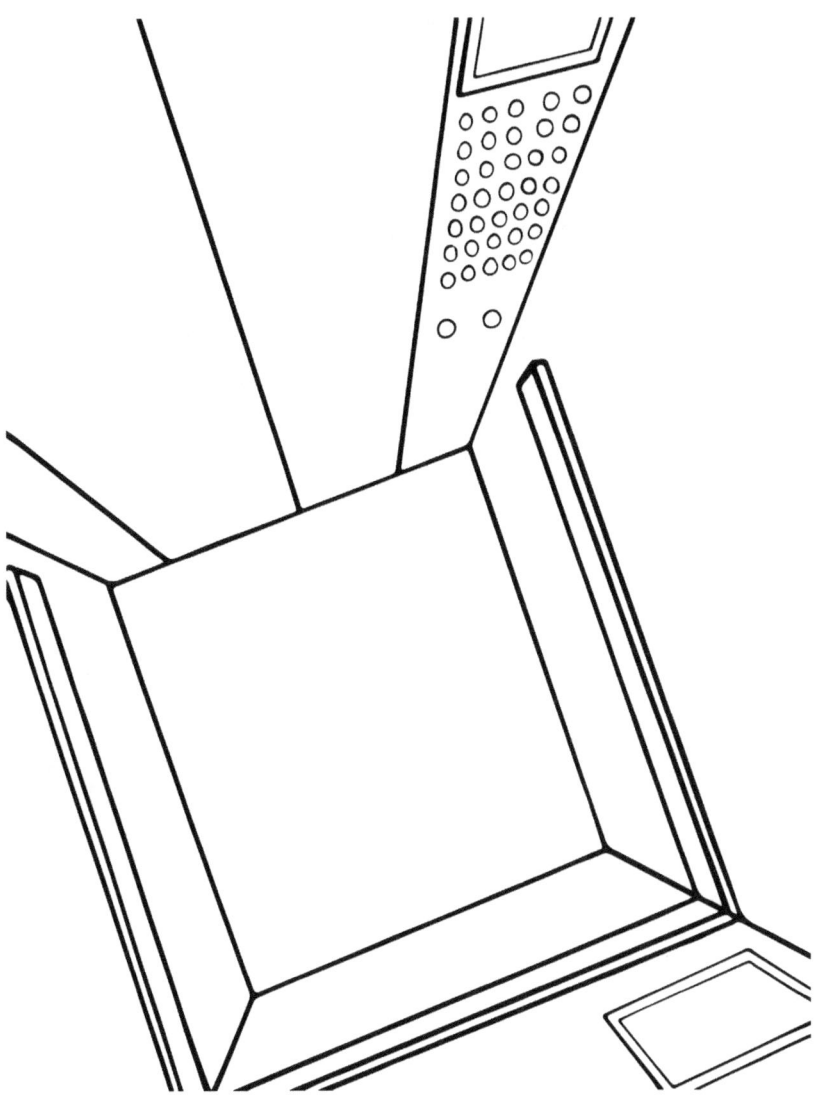

Afterward

Thank you for spending your time with this book. To continue your journey, please visit us to find out when the next volume will become available. Join in on the conversation and share your daydreams!

Only at

WWW.THEDAYDREAMBOOK.COM

www.ingramcontent.com/pod-product-compliance
Lightning Source LLC
LaVergne TN
LVHW051506070426
835507LV00022B/2957